Ager

GW01072028

An Expose of the United Nations' Sustainable Development Initiative and the Forfeiture of American Sovereignty and Liberties

Published in the United States

ISBN-13: 978-1530674442

ISBN-10: 1530674441

Table of Contents

New Age Dawning

There is a new age dawning in America and around the world that promises to change everything you know, as well as the values you hold dear.

The values we hold dear, like life, liberty, and the pursuit of happiness form the foundation of who we are as a people and a nation. Our traditions and laws are based on these values and were originally designed to preserve human dignity. In my opinion, human dignity is as vital to life as the air we breathe and the water we drink. Without it, life perishes. As you will discover in this book, proponents of Agenda 21 believe you are a nuisance. Your very existence represents a stumbling block to a master plan that equates human life to a colony of ants, where the rights of the individual and human dignity are defined by servitude, not freedom, and where personal ambition must be expended for the "greater good."

The assault on your dignity and rights will not take place in one fell swoop, but will be eroded one right at a time. It's like the proverbial salami that gets consumed one slice at a time. At first you don't notice your salami is shrinking as you hack off a slice and share it with a friend. But as one slice turns into two, and then three, you begin to notice a change. Eventually, your entire salami is gone. Agenda 21 is just one knife the United Nations and the U.S. Government is using to slice into your rights and gorge themselves at your expense. My opinions in this area are further supported by James Madison where he stated, "I believe there are more instances of the abridgement of the freedom of the people by gradual silent encroachments of those in power, than by violent and sudden usurpations."

And now, the United Nations has upped the ante by proposing 17 ambitious and politically motivated goals to bring peace to our cities, feed the hungry, house the poor, and cultivate your national abeyance. They call the plan the *2030 Agenda*. The 2030 Agenda represents a crucial escalation in the global assault on American sovereignty. For details, see the 2030 Agenda Appendix.

If you doubt the veracity of the United Nations' goal to run the world, consider the comments made by top delegates to the Cancun 2010 16th annual conference of the United Nations Framework Convention on Climate Change (UNFCCC). During the conference, newly appointed secretary for all things climate related, Christina Figueres, openly defined the proceedings a "litmus test for global governance" (Schlafly, 2010).

Throughout the proceedings, the resounding cry from under developed nations was a demand for cash payouts from developed nations, namely the United States, in the form of reparations for their carbon footprint and abuse of global natural resources. U.N. Secretary General Ban Ki-moon seconded this demand with a call "to fundamentally transform the global economy, based on low-carbon, clean-energy resources." Like it or not, the majority of the 194 signatories to the Agenda 21 plan are gunning for America.

The information in this book is not the stuff of conspiracy theorists or kooks, it is real. Everything I discuss in this book has been derived from official United Nations and U.S. Government published documents, which are readily available to the public. The elitists, world leaders, and self-appointed tin-pot gods make no attempt to hide their plans or activities. Why should they? To them, the masses are asses, too ignorant, lazy, and comfortable to risk upsetting the status quo or question the motives of a government run amok. Originally devised to regulate the global environment, the United Nations' Agenda 21 initiative, also known as Sustainable Development, has evolved into a political objective, calling for the complete subjugation of the world's population, including the people of the United States, through massive relocation of entire cities, depopulation, and the expansive cordoning of land into nature preserves.

Under Agenda 21 the common man takes a backseat to nature, freeing the elites and government figures to enjoy a pristine planet unspoiled by the unwashed masses. But this idyllic dream may only come to fruition where good men and women stand idle. As Medal of Honor recipient and author of the book "If Not Now, When,"

Colonel Jack Jacobs wrote, "complacency has an unpleasant habit of becoming perilous." We live in perilous times, and are entering an age where the realization of Karl Marx's ten planks to seize power (see Appendix A) are gaining momentum.

As you will learn in this book, Agenda 21 is not an urban legend. It is a fact of life, endorsed by our various presidents and put into motion through treaties and Executive Orders. Prepare yourself for the dawning of Agenda 21.

"When a man who is honestly mistaken hears the truth, he will either quit being mistaken, or cease to be honest."

Abraham Lincoln

Mission Accomplished

The United Nations is an incredibly complex organization, and has successfully intertwined its resources and regulations into every facet of life on Earth.

Like Winston Churchill's proverbial "riddle, wrapped in a mystery, inside an enigma," the United Nations has dispatched its tentacles around the world disguised as food programs, peacekeeping, free trade, economic development, and climate control, among others. Now, it has only to flex its long arms to suck the life out of national sovereignty and your freedoms.

In a macabre transfer of oppression, unelected ambassadors and underlings from under developed nations are allowed to organize committees and implement social change around the world in something akin to what Frederick Douglass called "the fatal poison of irresponsible power." Their favorite target: The United States of America. Back home the combined gross domestic product of these ambassador's nations rarely amount to much more than the annual budget of a school district in the U.S., but in the glass cage of the U.N. building in New York City, they move and act like gods.

These are the men and women to whom we may one day bow.

The United Nations was created in 1945 following World War II. Like most emerging bureaucracies, the United Nations' original charter sounded benign enough, and reflected the greatest concerns of the time—primarily the prevention of war. Chapter 1 of the United Nations charter discusses the four primary objectives of this international body:

To maintain international peace and security, and to that end: to take effective collective measures for the prevention and removal of threats to the peace, and for the suppression of acts of aggression or other breaches of the peace, and to bring about by peaceful means, and in conformity with the principles of justice and international law, adjustment or settlement of international disputes or situations which might lead to a breach of the peace;

To develop friendly relations among nations based on respect for the principle of equal rights and self-determination of peoples, and to take other appropriate measures to strengthen universal peace;

To achieve international co-operation in solving international problems of an economic, social, cultural, or humanitarian character, and in promoting and encouraging respect for human rights and for fundamental freedoms for all without distinction as to race, sex, language, or religion; and, to be a center for harmonizing the actions of nations in the attainment of these common ends.

The United Nations currently has 194 member states, each of which is allowed a single vote in the general assembly, including the United States. The organization as a whole divides its operations into five specific organs: General Assembly, Security Council, Economic and Social Council, Secretariat, and the International Court of Justice. The United Nations also sponsors several agencies, including the World Health Organization, World Food Program, International Atomic Energy Agency, Food and Agriculture Organization, World Bank, and the United Nations Children's Fund.

Since 1959 the John Birch Society has campaigned to get the United States out of the United Nations, claiming its true goal was the formation of a One World Government. Following the creation of the United Nations in 1945, U.S. State Department official J. Reuben Clark noted the United Nations charter did not ensure peace, but instead promoted war on the United Nations' terms. According to Clark, the United Nations was not designed to promote peace, but to control future wars by deciding who can declare war, who is allowed to engage in the fighting, and who has control over the troops doing the fighting. In other words, our future national sovereignty will be decided by the United Nations, not Congress (McManus, 2002).

Interestingly, the United Nations Charter was written by three men with ties to the Council on Foreign Relations and the Soviet Union—an organization and a nation devoted to communism and one world government. To achieve "one world government" status, the United Nations would need to succeed in implementing a world tax, gain judicial powers through a world court, and have a standing army to impose its will on recalcitrant members. During the 2010 Cancun climate summit, delegates pushed for a world tax to force nations to pay for carbon based resource usage, and its judicial authority has been established with the creation of the International Criminal Court established in 2002 and based in The Hague, Netherlands. As for a military, the United Nations has access to a standing army in the form of blue helmeted volunteers from member states.

The suggestion that the United Nations harbors a nefarious underlying mission has also been noted by people like Congressman John Rankin, who once stated, "The United Nations is the greatest fraud in history. Its purpose is to destroy the United States," and further led the U.N. World Constitution to note, "The age of nations must end. The governments of nations have decided to order their separate sovereignties into one government to which they will surrender their arms." And while the United Nations may claim it wishes only for world peace, its growing role in peacekeeping has allowed it to build, equip, and train a standing army.

Notably, the United Nations has led dozens of peacekeeping operations throughout its history, including operations in Korea, Bosnia, Haiti, Kosovo, Africa, and Cyprus, among others.

It should also be noted that peacekeeping is not a function of the United Nations, as defined by its charter. In my opinion this is yet another example of mission creep and is suggestive of how this international bureaucracy can stick its fingers into virtually anything it wants, and potentially dictate the behavior and rights of citizens in any country, including the United States. From a soldier's perspective this was evident during the Kosovo peacekeeping mission where the United Nations pressured President Bill Clinton to place U.S. troops under the command of the United Nations. Soldiers on the ground in Kosovo balked at this suggestion and flatly refused to exchange their helmets for the baby blue helmets worn by United Nations soldiers. This argument is based on widely held beliefs that the United Nations is a dangerous organization, determined to spread its one world government views at the expense of national sovereignty.

Another favorite area of the United Nations is free trade. As an expatriate living in various European and Asian countries, I saw firsthand the fallacy of free trade principles and challenged my Congressman to defend the principles of free trade with countries where the majority of the citizens made less than $200 per month. While American consumers can flock to big box department stores by the busload to buy cheap imported goods, on the other side of the pond consumers in poorer countries, with no disposable income, are fortunate enough to buy a bag of rice, much less an automobile manufactured in America.

To compound this problem, American manufacturers faced with rising labor costs, taxes, and prohibitive environmental laws, closed their stateside operations and moved their entire operations overseas. The result of this wholesale abandonment of America is evident in the major Rust Belt cities like Detroit, Pittsburgh, and Cleveland, and has transformed the major manufacturing power of the world into a nation of shopkeepers and hamburger flippers. But the transfer of manufacturing capacity to countries like Sri Lanka, Vietnam, and Malaysia were not necessarily godsends to the local people in these developing nations.

During a tour of 21 different garment factories in a Middle Eastern country, I observed the gross violation of human dignity and labor laws first hand. Men and women imported from sub-continent Asia worked in tin-roofed plants that resembled converted chicken coops. In many of these plants I could not even stand upright, and walked past rows upon rows of sewing machines operating in squalid conditions. Laborers were routinely bussed to the garment factory to work 12 hour shifts without a break, and then returned to concrete dwellings we would not put a convicted killer in. The $30 to $50 dollars each laborer earned monthly was reduced by living expenses, leaving them with a few dollars to send home to impoverished families. The product of their labor was unceremoniously boxed up for shipment to the United States, where star struck American consumers could purchase name brand designer clothing at cut rate prices.

South of the border, U.S. based companies are able to enjoy unfettered access to the U.S. market, courtesy of the North American Free Trade Agreement (NAFTA) while paying labor around 60 cents per hour and not putting up with environmental restrictions or invasive government inspections. In the lofty and deluded thinking of world free traders, the belief is a strong Mexican economy, bolstered at the expense of manufacturing in the U.S., will strengthen its resolve to protect the environment. Again, how can the U.S. laborer compete with this? And why would multi-national companies not exploit these overseas and cross-border opportunities with a vengeance? They owe no allegiance to America, and simply go wherever they wish in order to maximize shareholder value.

This is the reality of free trade.

Beyond concerns over free trade, national sovereignty, and the mission of the United Nations, this international body has also fallen suspect to major graft and corruption charges, which includes billions of dollars of unaccounted funds, pedophilia and rape of refugees in the Democratic Republic of Congo and other African nations, and most recently the apparent spread of cholera in Haiti (Williams, 2005).

Is it any wonder that people worry about the implementation of Agenda 21?

In Thailand, local implementation of sustainable development programs is facilitated by compensating locals to attend Agenda 21 meetings (Tonami & Mori, 2007). Tonami and Mori further point out that the long term prognosis for successful implementation of sustained development initiatives will hinge on continued support, presumably through incentives and top-down enforcement of participation. This so-called top-down participation implies resistance to Agenda 21 at the ground level, and further suggests local and national governments recognize Agenda 21 may be a hard sell. Perhaps the people know something about Agenda 21 that their governments choose to either ignore, or not share with their constituents.

The question of Agenda 21 efficacy at the local level was further challenged in the Caribbean, where an analysis of councils for sustained development in Grenada, Dominica, and St. Lucia found councils tend to dissipate when members are not incentivized to participate (Rosenberg & Thomas, 2005). Again, there is nothing like a government program that proclaims huge benefits to participants, but then must pay people to meet to discuss it. If Agenda 21 was such a good deal, people would naturally flock to its meetings and lead the way in ensuring its broad implementation.

Other than paying members of the public to support Agenda 21, municipal and national government bodies are finding people are resistant to change, or being inconvenienced by change, when that change benefits others. Norway is recognized as a pioneer in environmental initiatives, but even in this liberal nation, government leaders have found resistance to the global perspective of Agenda 21 (Aal, 2000). Instead, Norwegians embrace local initiatives that provide visible results and benefits to their localities. As in American political elections, politics surrounding Agenda 21 appear to be local. Ironically, it is this very provincialism the United Nations is striving to circumvent in its global sustained development initiative.

Overall, this resistance to change, and the public demand for direct compensation to participate in Agenda

21 programs, bodes well for the demise of sustained development. However, the United Nations is determined to impose their one world view and one world government on the rest of us, despite our misgivings. If they succeed, their idea of utopia may well become our idea of Hell on Earth.

"A lie can travel halfway around the world while the truth is putting on its shoes."

Mark Twain

U.S. Government Complicity

There is no doubt the United States government is a signatory to the Agenda 21 initiative, but perhaps the most galling aspect of this complicity to subvert national sovereignty in the name of environment is the zeal our own representatives and elected officials from the local to the state and federal levels have for this United Nations' driven usurpation.

In addition to the illustrations portrayed in this document, a recent court ruling suggests just how far the federal government will go to facilitate the implementation of Agenda 21, despite populist objection to its implications.

On 17 December, 2013, U.S. District Court Judge Ellen Huvelle ruled the President's "executive privilege" did not extend to communications beyond his inner circle. At question: A presidential directive dictating how federal government agencies should interpret and implement aspects of his previously published Presidential Policy Directive on Global Development.

In an 8 page PDF file, available at https://www.fas.org/irp/offdocs/ppd/global-dev.pdf , published in 2010. At the heart of this document is a U.S. taxpayer funded foreign assistance program designed to lock in global cooperation in various green initiatip0oslaa,mves, including named programs like Feed the Future, Global Health Initiative, and Global Climate Change Initiative.

The President's directive on global development, formally known as the Presidential Policy Directive on Global Development, cites the federal government's sustainable development efforts as a "strategic, economic, and moral imperative" (Presidential Directive, 2010, pg 1).

The directive further uses "national security" as justification for leading the industrialized world in restricting development and implementing Agenda 21 policies at the risk of violating every American citizen's private property rights and economic freedoms.

According to this Presidential Directive, the United States will, "Elevate development as a central pillar of our national security policy, equal to diplomacy and defense, and build and integrate the capabilities that can advance our interests" (Presidential Directive, 2010, pg 5). In other words, through USAID and other gift giving agencies of the federal government, we will not only impose development restrictions on U.S. citizens, but will further the scourge of managed development to the entire world—courtesy of U.S. taxpayer dollars.

Don't under estimate the power of the United Nations' Agenda 21 initiative to adversely impact your life as it strips American citizens of constitutional guarantees and compromises our national sovereignty. The remainder of this document will illustrate how the U.S. government is facilitating the implementation of this U.N. initiative, and what you can do about it.

As far as the general public gaining access to the President's document related to global development and international aid—don't hold your breath.

Hell in a Nutshell

It is hard to predict exactly what the future may hold, but it is possible to make accurate extrapolations based on current events, political agendas, and documented objectives of government bodies. Frankly, I'm worried.

Hell as I see it is the forfeiture of my human dignity and constitutional rights at the hands of a governing body. I served with the U.S. military in two combat zones, and have two sons who currently serve in the U.S. Army; yet one day the soldiers I once revered and called my friends may become my enemy as they follow the orders of their appointed commanders and march on the cities and homes of private citizens in the United States and other developed nations around the world. And it does not take Nostradamus to foretell this future. You need only step back to New Orleans 2005 to observe American soldiers forcefully collecting weapons from law abiding citizens and removing people from their homes to relocation centers and FEMA trailer camps to see the future.

The quiet acceptance of these acts was deafening and is a harbinger of things to come when the U.S. government capitulates to the United Nations. In fact, we may have already done so, as evidenced by President George H.W. Bush's comments to the United Nations General Assembly where he stated, "It is the sacred principles enshrined in the United Nations Charter to which the American people will henceforth pledge their allegiance." What are those "sacred principles?" And, do they conflict with the principles set forth in the Constitution many of us have sworn to protect and defend?

Following the Constitutional Convention of 1789, Benjamin Franklin notably remarked "You have a republic, if you can keep it." Like many of our Founding Fathers, Franklin knew all too well the ease by which tyranny could destroy freedom, and how ordinary men can lose sight of their moral compass in the glare of power. One hundred years later Lord Acton famously echoed Franklin's cynicism for power when he stated, "Power tends to corrupt, and absolute power corrupts absolutely. Great men are almost always bad men." It is easy to forget that government leaders are flesh and blood, blessed with the same vices of avarice and vanity as the rest of us; and left unchecked, it is these very shortcomings that will be our undoing. In my opinion Agenda 21 is the height of hubris, a product of leaders left to govern without the consent of the governed.

The fruition of Agenda 21 is an Orwellian world of restricted travel, complete lack of privacy, deprivation of human dignity, and subjugation to totalitarian rule. Is this an exaggeration? Is it possible for a nation to usurp natural law and repeal everything we have fought for from the Magna Carta to the Constitution? Think about it. We have already sold ourselves into slavery in the name of safety, consumerism, and entertainment, and have furthered the cause of despotism by allowing fear to dictate our values and beliefs. Is it any great leap for a government to take the next step in population control and resort to coercion to implement its global objectives through eugenics, euthanasia, and concentration camps? And, is the veiled "papers please" reference to Nazism that much different than the Department of Homeland Security's current "viper" policies? Or, as Zbigniew Brzezinski once wrote, governments use "terror as a deliberate tool of political intimidation" to enact laws, gain power, and usurp human rights in the name of safety—which leads me back to Benjamin Franklin and his warning that any society that allows its rights to be taken away in the name of safety, deserves neither rights, nor safety.

Americans want nothing more than a sweet taste in their mouths and a few hours of mindless drivel on television to wash it down. And this passion for comfort, safety, and diversion will be our undoing.

By now I hope you are asking yourself one or two questions: namely, how did we get to this point? And, what can be done about it?

"There is nothing more frightening than active ignorance."

Goethe

A Fine Kettle of Fish

We have reached this point because of a collective failure to care.

Somewhere along the line we abdicated our rights to govern ourselves, and placed the future of this republic in the hands of elected and appointed officials, who for the most part would not qualify for a minimum wage job in a soda shop. But we hired them anyway, entrusted them with the store's cash drawer, and gave them the key to the Executive Washroom.

In some ways the roots of our problems may be traced to Franklin Roosevelt's New Deal, Lyndon Johnson's Great Society, or perhaps even the National Security Act of 1947, that cumulatively bred an entitlement mentality among the citizenry and authorized the debasement of individual rights and privacy. But the truth may actually lie closer to home, where individual apathy and egocentricity drives one to believe his or her obligations to governance ends at the ballot box. A recent example of this point is evident in Bell, California, where a host of city managers and council members defrauded a small, blue-collar community of millions in exorbitant salaries and questionable contracts. A vigilant electorate would have never allowed this to happen.

Compounding the voter apathy issue, state and local referendums are frequently overruled by judges who choose to legislate from the bench. For example, in California a recent proposition to block official sanctioning of same-sex marriages won the majority of votes cast. However, immediately following the election, supporters of same-sex marriages appealed to the courts for injunctions against the referendum. In a state of nearly 40 million people, one judge overruled the will of the majority of voters. Similar scenarios are played out across the country in case after case, eroding voter confidence in the system and further disenfranchising the citizen's role in self-governance. To answer Benjamin Franklin's challenge, it is impossible to maintain a republic when the voter is powerless.

In his 2009 address to the United Nations General Assembly, President Obama declared four things are critical to the future of the world's population: "nonproliferation and disarmament; the promotion of peace and security; the preservation of our planet; and a global economy that advances opportunity for all people." Obama does not seem to be much different than other presidents in this regard, but his drive to recognize the United Nations as the facilitator in these four areas suggests he is willing to allow the United States to kowtow to the wishes of an international body, rather than those of the American electorate. This is especially worrisome in light of his executive powers (see Appendix B: Executive Orders).

Years ago I worked for a nationally recognized chain restaurant. The restaurant employed an array of control mechanisms that required tickets for every hamburger that left the kitchen, and following each shift servers matched every food ticket used against printed receipts to verify payment. The movement of two dollar plates of burgers and fries from the kitchen to the customer was controlled like gold transfers at Fort Knox.

Yet, our local, state, and federal government bodies handle billions of dollars and make life changing decisions for the governed with no apparent oversight, and even societal changing laws like the Obama Health Care Reform Bill are enacted without having been read or debated while 70 percent of the population clamored for details.

This same neglect and crass disregard for the democratic process emboldened leaders at the United Nations to impose Agenda 21 on the world.

"When a well-packaged web of lies has been sold gradually to the masses over generations, the truth will seem utterly preposterous and its speaker a raving lunatic."

Dresden James

The Proof is in the Pudding

The next section takes Agenda 21 and the sustained development initiatives of the United Nations out of the realm of conspiracy and into the world of reality. In the following pages I will review key elements of the two documents mentioned above and share my opinion of how they are being implemented across our society today.

"Agenda 21: United Nations Sustainable Development" was created during the 1992 Rio de Janeiro Conference on Environment & Development, and was signed by 178 nations, including President George H.W. Bush. Following its approval, President Bill Clinton signed Executive Order 12852 in 1993, creating the President's Council on Sustainable Development, which in turn has created numerous documents relevant to Agenda 21, including the 170 page document, "Towards a Sustainable America: Advancing Prosperity, Opportunity, and a Healthy Environment for the 21st Century," published in 1999.

The title "Agenda 21" refers to the 21st Century, and as the name implies, sets forth an agenda for controlling development throughout the world. This 351 page document is divided into three sections and 40 chapters.

- Section 1: Social and Economic Dimensions

- Section 2: Conservation and Management of Resources for Development

- Section 3: Strengthening the Role of Major Groups

The Preamble sets forth the vision of the sustained development initiative as a global partnership, where all nations must cooperate to eradicate hunger, poverty, illiteracy, and ill-health. As you can see, in the first paragraph of this document, the United Nations has expanded the vision of climate and environment control to include the health, safety, and education of the world's population. It is this type of "mission creep" that is dangerous, as bureaucracies are created to implement the Agenda 21 vision, and each bureaucracy expands its reach, budget, and goals.

While the U.N. acknowledges Agenda 21 is a global initiative, the Preamble further stresses the need for national governments to ensure proper plans, strategies, policies, and processes are put into place to pave the way for global implementation. Of course, America led the charge on this when President Clinton signed Executive Order 12852. The U.N. further invites non-governmental agencies to join the fray, and suggests the goals of the initiative may change as circumstances and needs change over time. In other words, "we're not entirely sure what we want, but we'll let you know when the time comes."

Call me mean spirited, but the entire gist of the Agenda 21 agreement sounds like a contrived way to reduce America's strength by transferring its human and material resources, as well as wealth and technologies, to developing nations. In short, they want to take 230 years' worth of profits and hard work (derived from our successful free enterprise system), and give it away to people, nations, and cultures that cannot produce for themselves. Given the graft and corruption rampant throughout the world, and their respective embracing of failed governmental systems, this seems like an incredible waste.

This zero-sum view of the world is reflective of the values and beliefs of key players in the United Nations who firmly believe the only way for an under developed nation to get ahead is to redistribute technology and wealth from the developed nations. This fallacy totally disregards the role of private enterprise, innovation, and human ingenuity to create, and in fact compounds the problem by utilizing public, rather than private, distribution models. Additionally, while the United Nations promotes the transference of private property into the public domain for preservation, many economists believe the roots of personal and national wealth may be found in the privatization of property and industry. Ironically, government officials who extoll the benefits of moving private property into public trusts for the good are the same people who have failed abysmally in their mission to create peace on earth and end world hunger. What makes them think they could manage businesses and the private lives of people?

Leading the charge to assume control of private property, the Agenda 21 has set its sights on technology. Agenda 21 represents a wholesale give away of our technology and patents to developing nations, and in fact clearly states developing nations should receive "favored" status as recipients of technology from developed nations. The idea is that we should all have access to state of the art technologies in the name of environmental safety. While it sounds good on the surface, what it amounts to is placing all nations on a level playing field technologically. Of course, I may be old fashioned, or perhaps a bit ethnocentric, but I like the fact that U.S. technology is superior and is of strategic importance to our national security. According to Agenda 21, "environmentally sound technologies are not just individual technologies, but total systems which include know-how, procedures, goods and services, and equipment as well as organizational and managerial procedures."

Well Hell, why don't we just do the work for them also?

To facilitate this transfer of knowledge, the U.N. would sanction clearing houses to process requests for technologies using joint ventures and partnerships. In other words, the U.N. would decide who gets what information, and how it is used. In a head nod to intellectual and proprietary properties, the U.N. states a system would need to be created to ensure property owners are compensated for their technologies, using "fiscal or otherwise" means.

The United Nations' sustained development initiative will change your life.

Reading the 351 page Agenda 21 document is like peeling an onion, where each successive layer reveals yet another layer of treachery. It begins harmlessly enough by extolling the benefits of climate control and how the Agenda 21 plan will save us all from certain doom. After all, global warming is killing people in third world nations, burying entire islands in the South Pacific, melting glaciers in Nepal, and choking the air with industrial waste. As you peel away the Preamble layer, lofty platitudes become specific plans to depopulate the world, relocate millions of people into centralized mega-cities, indoctrinate children in government sponsored re-education centers, and confiscate broad swaths of private property.

At the surface Agenda 21 looks like a benign plan to improve the quality of life on earth and preserve its precious resources for future generations. But at the core, in my opinion, is the apparent malignant kernel of the United Nations' true objective—control.

Am I exaggerating? Never under estimate the United Nations' resolve to govern the world through sustained development, and the U.S. Government's acquiescence, to its implementation. During the 2010 Cancun Climate Summit, U.N. Secretary-General Ban Ki-moon, expressed "deep concern" over the slow progress being made in implementing sustained development initiatives around the world, and proclaimed, "We need results now." In an oft repeated strategy, Ban concluded by asking once again for more money from the developed nations, implying the United States is not doing enough to speed its own reconstruction in the image of Agenda 21. Apparently, the radicals are getting impatient with the slow progress of Agenda 21, and are chagrined by the popular revolt against their blueprint for a new world order.

As a signatory to Agenda 21, the United States has accepted the provisions laid out in this document, and has furthered its implementation through Executive Order, various regulations, and the publication of its seminal document "Towards a Sustainable America."

It is time to wake up and stop the madness.

In a hilarious documentation of the United Nations' apparent ignorance of science, and its blatant distain for all things American, delegates to the Cancun 2010 Climate Summit were asked to sign two separate "spoof" petitions (CFACT, 2010). One petition asked for support in derailing the U.S. economy for its failure to support the Kyoto Protocol by taking action to reduce the United States' gross domestic product by 6 percent, while the second petition fooled virtually every delegate they asked to ban water because it is a major component in acid rain. I'm not too bothered by the attendee's support of a water ban. After all, this is just indicative of their stupidity: however, when they support a cause that calls for the destruction of the U.S. economy, that's outrageous, and indicative of their true motives.

Agenda 21 is round one of an inflection point in globalization where local and national governments will increasingly defer their role in governance to a world body. This trend is evident where the 1992 Rio Summit laid the ground work for sustained development, which led to President Clinton's Executive Order in 1993 that established the President's Council on Sustainable Development. Using their presidential charter, the council immediately created a framework for pushing the sustainable development concept to the local level.

At the local level professional facilitators are enlisted to organize and facilitate Town Hall, or focus group, meetings to discuss the local implementation of environmental policies in accordance with the sustained development model. While local community activists believe they are affecting policy, they are actually falling into the facilitator's snare, which in effect serves the master plan laid out by the United Nations in Rio, and not those of Pretoria or Yorba Linda.

If you have ever attended a focus group or Town Hall event, you know the facilitator has already chosen the topic for discussion. For example, a typical discussion in rural Montana may revolve around the idea of protecting the habitat of the dwindling wolverine population. From there, the facilitator typically selects three options available for debate, which typically includes two extreme options on opposite ends of the political or environmental spectrum, and one, middle of the road option, that in actuality is the facilitator's desired choice. In this case, participants in the meeting may be asked to discuss whether the community should support ignoring the issue and allowing Darwin to be in the driver's seat; using eminent domain to seize private property and open corridors of protected habitat for the wolverines, or implementing a local policy regarding development and sprawl that will protect the wolverine's habitat at current levels.

The first two choices represent extremes that have little hope of gaining support at any level, but the third choice, which ironically is the choice of the facilitator, gains support as the only viable option. Following a round table (we're all so equal) discussion the participants agree to champion the cause of restricted development of their lands and leave the session feeling proud to have participated in the policy making process in their community.

The entire process is a sham, carefully orchestrated by professionals who play local crowds like a fiddle to achieve their objectives. Here are some actual examples of how this process has impacted various communities across the nation.

Always willing to lead the way in radical reform, San Francisco enacted a composting ordinance that authorizes fines of up to $500 for placing organic items like orange peels, coffee grounds, and even greasy food wrappers, in the trash. I guess we are supposed to store our greasy pizza boxes under the bed, or perhaps return them to the pizzeria for the next customer's use. Communities across the nation followed the San Francisco example and have since enacted aggressive recycling and landfill usage laws that promise to micro-manage every aspect of your resource usage.

As a California native I have also noted with disgust how environmental reform often comes at the expense of business and property owners. For example, farmers in the San Joaquin Valley depend on irrigation to grow a huge chunk of America's fruits, nuts, and vegetables. But, restrictions on water usage due to an endangered fish in the San Joaquin River delta area has created a manmade drought throughout the valley and stopped food production on thousands of acres. Likewise, in Riverside County homeowners have been threatened with steep fines and jail sentences if they clear the brush around their homes. Apparently, a local critter akin to vermin called the kangaroo rat depends upon the brush for its survival. Brush fires in the area have subsequently destroyed millions of dollars-worth of homes and structures that would otherwise have avoided fire damage. One homeowner blamed her home's destruction on bureaucrats that placed the safety of a rat over humans. Sadly, the same fire that destroyed many homes also burned the rats.

Not to be outdone, the Occupation, Safety, and Health Administration (OSHA) jumped on the environmental bandwagon in 1995 with its new ban on lead based paint in residential facilities. OSHA used quasi-science to justify its ban by dosing rats with huge wallops of lead on a daily basis, and then extrapolating the results to suggest much smaller doses of lead would be harmful to humans. Sure, lead and other heavy metals may pose risks to humans, but let's at least compare apples to apples in our research methodologies. If OSHA used the same research regimen for other chemicals and materials, up to 50 percent of everything humans manufacture and use in their daily lives would be banned. Interestingly, the OSHA ban on lead impacts homes built prior to 1978, and its demands for hazardous homes to be destroyed or vacated suggests a means towards the ends regarding the wholesale relocation of populations, as discussed below.

Anti-human environmental reform poses a real threat to economic development at the local level—which oddly enough seems to suit the United Nations' sustained development objectives very well. Communities that can no longer build manufacturing facilities; homeowners that cannot manage their private property; and citizens that cannot find work or afford to adhere to environmental laws, must die, or at least blow away. The realization of up to 50 percent of the land mass in the continental United States being removed from human habitation or use is just a handful of environmental regulations away.

Information is power, and in my opinion nothing derails a despot's malicious plot like transparency and public awareness. The next time you participate in a local political event or focus group, pay attention to how the discussion is manipulated by the facilitator. Keep your eyes and mind open, and refuse to be corralled by professionals bent on roping you into predetermined conclusions that will threaten your private property rights and limit your personal freedoms.

Long before Ronald Reagan became President of the United States, he delivered a speech to the Phoenix Chamber of Commerce in 1961, where he revealed a basic tenet in his philosophy of freedom and the American way of life. Reagan stated, "Freedom is never more than one generation away from extinction. We didn't pass it on to our children in the bloodstream. It must be fought for, protected, and handed on for them to do the same, or one day we will spend our sunset years telling our children what it was once like in the United States when men were free." It is this "one generation" that advocates for sustainable development target when they champion education reform.

A leading educational philosopher, Benjamin Bloom, proudly proclaims education is a process of changing a student's thoughts, actions, and feelings. According to Bloom, this is best accomplished by challenging his or her belief system. At the root of this educational reform is a drive to reduce the role of the individual in society in deference to the needs of the community. This so-called educational reform teaches our children the values of the new world order in place of real education. As Charlotte Iserbyt, a former Department of Education Senior Advisor, posits in her book "The Deliberate Dumbing Down of America," that environmentalists believe educated people consume more resources than uneducated people. Therefore, to reduce consumption and achieve sustainable development, we must simply offer educational opportunities that focus on values, rather than facts.

This educational reform initiative is evident in the UNESCO program called "United Nations' Decade of

Education for Sustainable Development." It is their stated goal in this program to steal one generation of children and teach them to place loyalty to the state above loyalty to the family. Once this objective has been realized, it is a simple task to then inculcate the children with the basic tenets of sustainable development. These tenets include:

- End of national sovereignty

- Abolition of private property

- Restructuring of the family unit

- Restriction of individual mobility and opportunity

- Abandonment of constitutional rights

- Relocation of people into smart growth zones

In the next few sections we will discuss each of these tenets in more detail and reveal how this pervasive slippery slope to tyranny is rapidly overtaking the American way of life. Remember Ronald Reagan's words. If we allow the United Nations' Agenda 21 to take root in our society, life as we know it is finished.

End of National Sovereignty

As long as nations stand alone, the United Nations will not be able to fully implement its one world government plans.

Throughout this book I have talked about how the United Nations has written a detailed environmental plan for worldwide implementation. The plan is then pushed down to the national and local levels, where rules and regulations are enacted allowing United Nations' oversight. It is a slippery slope towards a new world order.

For example, when the United Nations asks nations to reduce carbon emissions by 25 percent, the practical implications of this goal becomes restrictions on fossil fuel power generation plants, closure of coal mines, reduction of gross domestic products, and limitations on economic development, among a host of others. When nations defer these decisions and rulings to the United Nations, they effectively abdicate their national sovereignty to the dictators and tyrants of the world.

Abolition of private property

The cornerstone of America's success is the protection of private property. The pursuit of property motivates individuals to take risks, be innovative, and protect the social and legal structure that preserves his or her private property. Without the protection of our private property, the will to achieve or build something worthwhile in this world would evaporate quicker than a politician's campaign promises.

When you think of private property, do not limit your vision to a stake of land out in the country. Private property is also the patents and copyrights you may hold, the shares in your stock market portfolio, the car you drive, the business you own, and the home you live in.

One assault on private property is the so-called "Death Tax," also known as the Estate Tax. Currently, the Estate Tax is set at 35 percent, but this rate is under constant assault by the wealth re-distributors in Washington. Whether you have estate worth taxing or not, think about the injustice of this tax. Most personal estates are built on income derived from employment or investment income. That means the money used to build an estate has already been taxed by the government. Following your death, the government wants to tax you again. In my opinion, this is a deliberate act by our government to redistribute wealth and destroy private property.

To succeed in taking control of America, the United Nations must do something about private property rights in

America. The primary tools used to achieve this goal will be the re-zoning of property in the name of habitat preservation, land use restrictions imposed by new regulations governing development, and heavy taxation of proceeds from private property, such as the Death Tax and Capital Gains Tax. Additional encroachments will come in the form of eminent domain seizures, and outrageously expensive insurance premiums based on manufactured risk assessments.

Progress in this area seems slow, but never forget that the United Nations is patient—to a certain extent. They are willing to wait for you to die to take what you own. In my opinion, things will get dicey when they get impatient and devise ways to speed up the process—like government imposed healthcare and chemically laced food and water (but those are two separate conspiracies).

Restructuring of the family unit

According to the website unesco.org, "The United Nations Decade of Education for Sustainable Development (2005-2014), for which UNESCO is the lead agency, seeks to integrate the principles, values, and practices of sustainable development into all aspects of education and learning, in order to address the social, economic, cultural and environmental problems we face in the 21st century."

UNESCO has identified 8 themes it must dedicate itself to in their so-called Decade of Education:

1. Sustainable Urbanization

2. Sustainable Consumption

3. Peace and Human Security

4. Rural Development

5. Cultural Diversity

6. Gender Equality

7. Health Promotion

8. Environment

As is typical in any bureaucracy, you may note a considerable amount of duplication in the above themes. For example, Peace and Human Security sounds a lot like the U.N. peacekeeping mission, and its Health Promotion and Gender Equality themes appear to duplicate the missions of other U.N. agencies, like the U.N. Information and Resources on Gender Equality, and the World Health Organization. But duplication of effort and over kill is easy on somebody else's dime. Besides, the redundancy has a numbing effect on people, and lends credibility to the message when it is spread from multiple sources at the same time.

Under the auspices of the United Nations, education will "challenge us all to adopt new behaviors and practices," and will focus on holistic, rather than subject-based learning, and an emphasis on values rather than subject matter. UNESCO further notes that education must instill critical thinking among students, which sounds good on the surface, but is actually a euphemism for "values clarification. Under values clarification, students are taught there is no absolute right or wrong, which inevitably leads to the destruction of morality, the family unit, and our free society. For example, young students are now taught how to contact child protective services and other authorities if they believe their parents are abusing them. Again, on the surface this sounds admirable, but in practice it has led to many cases where justifiable discipline in the home has led to court ordered separation of children from their families. In another example of values clarification, students are taught that petty theft of food items is acceptable to alleviate hunger, especially where a poor child steals a food item from a "wealthy" grocer.

These value clarification lessons often take form in role playing, where a child may play the role of a greedy shopkeeper who physically abuses a child who has been caught stealing a candy bar. The shoplifter is generally portrayed as poor and disadvantaged, while the shopkeeper is wealthy and privileged. Of course, in this role playing scenario, the impressionable minds of 5-8 year old children sides with the thief. In practice, the values learned in this role playing scenario lead to a softening of societal pressures against aberrant behavior, and weaken the structure of a society based on lawful and moral behavior.

In another example of values clarification at work, students in London went on a rampage to protest hikes in college tuition. Their cause may be legitimate, but the destruction of public and private property, as well as the assault on innocent bystanders, including Prince Charles, is abhorrent, and reeks of humanistic values. After all, isn't class warfare a justifiable means towards the collective, equality for all, ends?

Why would the federal government implement values clarification training? And, why would UNESCO and the Agenda 21 program want to redefine the belief systems of children around the world? In my opinion there is only one reason: By destroying the moral fabric of a society they can instill their values and beliefs in their place.

As Charlotte Iserbyt noted in her book "The Deliberate Dumbing Down of America," the new model of education will teach students the values of collectivism and loyalty to the state over family and individual. All I can say is, thank God my kids were home-schooled.

Restriction of individual mobility and opportunity

If the globalists have their way, you will not have the need or right to own a car, or choose to travel cross-country without their permission. In this scenario, only the elite will have access to private modes of transportation.

The government preferred mode of transportation in the new world order is trains. As PJ O' Rourke notes, railroad tracks are a great way to control where people go and when they get there. Of course, cars are a big no-no in the new world order, as they afford freedom of movement and privacy.

During the December 2010 student riots in London, government officials shut down Tube stops and stations in the area of the riot, effectively blocking access to the area for people constrained to this mode of travel. Here in America, similar moves would be ineffectual, as only a small percentage of our population depends upon rail travel. But this may all change soon, as high speed rail projects are gearing up for a massive shift in how Americans travel.

Can you imagine being forced to travel by Amtrak, or staying home? A friend of mine recently travelled from Central California to Oklahoma City, via Amtrak. When he returned he told me the horrors of cross-country rail travel. Many of the major cities required transferring to buses to travel across breaks in the Amtrak service, and a transfer in San Antonio meant a 14 hour delay. Despite any effort by our government to impose rail travel on its citizenry, I can foresee a nightmare of travel delays, compounded by limited access to the places you may want to go. And in my opinion, this will be by design. If you live on the West Coast your movement across the fruited valley will be limited to railheads in San Diego, Los Angeles, San Francisco, and Seattle. Sadly, you would simply not have any business elsewhere. And your passion for motorcycling across the Mojave Desert, picnicking beneath El Capitan in Yosemite, or hiking the Sierra Crest Trail, will be verboten.

As a servant to the world's elite, you will live in a high rise apartment building within one mile of your work, and everything you need will be available within a short walk. Am I dreaming? This is the reality of life for many people in major cities across America already, so the actual restriction on their rights to travel outside their allocated smart growth zone will be virtually painless. I have a friend who has lived in an apartment in New York City his entire life. He does not own a car, takes the subway to work, and has his groceries delivered to his home. He loves it.

This lifestyle is totally foreign to those of us who grew up in rural America. We want room to roam, and the freedom to choose when and where we grow. For us, the change will be painful and will represent a severe curtailment of our constitutional rights. And for the entrepreneurs among us, Agenda 21 will severely limit your opportunities to start or run a business. They may never tell you outright that you do not have the right to operate a business; however, the permits and licenses to operate your business legally will be so onerous and expensive, the results will not be worth the effort. In this world of low initiative and reliance upon government for food, housing, healthcare, and jobs, the pioneer spirit that has built America will shrivel and die. In my hometown a local stock car race track has been in operation since the 1950s. At the time the track was built its location was miles outside the city and far away from any homes. Since then, homes have been built around it, and residents of the area have won so many zoning changes that the rack can only operate for a few hours per night, on one night of the week.

Similarly, a home site in a remote area of the Mojave Desert has been made uninhabitable because naturalists have been able to restrict the use of a natural water spring that fed the house with drinking water. The house sits empty today and is a testament to gradual forced migration of people off of the land and into the cities.

Ironically, the President's Council on Sustainable Development lists employment opportunities as the first key characteristic of sustainable development. In a business environment where innovation and development is severely limited, the only source of jobs I can think of must be the public sector. Again, this will be by design, as the surest route to government control of your life is your dependence on that government.

Abandonment of constitutional rights

The erosion of constitutional rights in the United States will never happen in one fell swoop. Instead, we will experience the gradual erosion of our rights as various real or manufactured crises demand.

Following the 9/11 tragedy, Congress and the President moved quickly to ensure government agencies had the capability to collect intelligence on potential terrorists. The end result became what is known as The Patriot Act.

The Patriot Act was enacted by Congress and signed into law by President George Bush on October 26, 2001— just weeks after the 9/11 event. The name "Patriot" is actually a cleverly devised acronym which stands for Providing Appropriate Tools Required to Intercept and Obstruct Terrorism.

Specifically, the act significantly reduced the restrictions placed on law enforcement agencies in the area of search and seizure operations, including electronic eavesdropping, email surveillance and cell phone monitoring. Additionally, the Patriot Act dramatically increased the monitoring of financial records and expanded surveillance of suspected terrorist activity to include domestic activities and immigration that critics believe significantly infringe upon civil and constitutional rights.

In my opinion, the most controversial aspect of this law is how it expanded the definition of domestic terrorism to include any activity deemed "dangerous to human life that are a violation of the criminal laws of the United States or of any State." Under this definition, virtually any suspected criminal could fall under the rules of the Patriot Act, effectively nullifying any due processes required under the Constitution.

A strong offense is the best defense against terrorism if we are to survive as a republic. However, I am beginning to wonder if we can achieve this without completely forfeiting our individual rights and freedoms to the government. Former FBI Director J. Edgar Hoover once bragged he could find a way to arrest any male citizen of the country. With the Patriot Act, he may have gotten his way.

Again, the Patriot Act is, in my opinion, an example of gradualism at work. Never one to waste a crisis, the federal government used the tragedy of 9/11 to implement search and seizure tools against its own citizens that prior to 9/11 we would never have been allowed. This same methodology of gradualism is at work in our transportation sector where the Department of Homeland Security is taken its safety mandate to new levels of civil rights encroachment.

In my opinion, the terrorists holed up in their wretched bat caves around the world are cheering the new security measures employed by the Transportation Security Agency (TSA). It must bust their guts to see Americans standing in line for naked body scanning and invasive body searches for the privilege of travelling from one city to another in this "free" country.

Terrorists despise our liberties, and count any mission to deprive us of our life, liberty, and pursuit of happiness as a resounding success. Sadly, in the name of "safety," our government appears over eager to accommodate the terrorists through placation, political correctness, and pandering, rather than the distasteful but necessary annihilation of any enemy to the people of this country. Instead, we have a federal government led by a man even the French and Germans declare as "too liberal," and dangerously socialist in his belief system.

Airline and airport security is a monumental undertaking, fraught with weak links and vulnerabilities. Think about it. An airport like LAX in Los Angeles is a city within a city, with an astonishing 56 million passengers arriving and departing annually, over 1.5 million tons of cargo handled each year, and approximately 544,000 flights per year. How many mechanics, cargo handlers, support personnel, and food service providers does it take to support an air hub of this size? And does each catering and/or maintenance truck accessing the airport secure area receive a pat down or image scan comparable to the flying passenger's regimen?

Have you ever shipped a package across country via airmail? Who do you think transports these packages? If you guessed commercial airlines, you would be right. There are U.S. Mail bags in virtually every aircraft crossing the fruited plains of this nation. Does each package shipped via airmail receive the same scrutiny as the passengers? I hope so, but kind of doubt it.

My point is, passengers are just the tip of the iceberg when it comes to airline security, and any terrorist smart enough to build a bomb knows this. Consider the recent incidents of explosives being shipped via air cargo carriers out of Yemen, bound for the UK and US. We always seem to thwart these shenanigans by the skin of our teeth, courtesy of a whistle blower. But what happens when our luck runs out?

There are no easy answers when it comes to airline security. Obviously, the government must take steps to protect safety of flight, but the TSA and Department of Homeland Security appears arrogant and disdainful of the flying public—and that is what irks me.

I hate to wave the white flag when it comes to exercising my rights, but in this case I am personally avoiding airports and flying as much as possible. I have cancelled vacation trips that required flying, and will continue to limit my exposure to what I perceive as the abusive power of a government agency, and invite you to reconsider supporting a system that blatantly disregards your constitutional rights. In my opinion, the current TSA protocol for screening passengers is nothing but window dressing, designed to instill confidence in the system, and train American citizens to accept the deprivation of their rights in the name of safety. Airport security, and the abuses of power by control hungry amateurs, is this generation's Alamo. We have to stop the violation of our constitutional rights before big government interprets acquiescence as permission to extend their invasive police tactics to every street corner in America.

One recent incident supports by contention of security risks among airport support personnel. According to the article "Skycap Scam Discovered at Miami International Airport," by Jade Walker, 15 baggage handlers have allegedly accepted cash payments from passengers to load their bags onto planes without going through the normal check-in procedure. While the motive appears purely profit oriented, circumventing the routine check-in and security screenings may pose significant safety of flight risks (Walker, 2010). Again, in my opinion passengers appear to garner the most attention from TSA personnel and procedures, while the behind the scenes activities in our airports operate with impunity.

Don't agree? Fine. Go ahead and subject your mother and daughter to the humiliation of the TSA groin grope. Just count me out.

You may have noticed that the above violations of our constitutional rights are at the hands of our own government and not the United Nations. As the saying goes, "With friends like these, who needs enemies?" My fear of the United Nations in this area stems from a historical pattern of our government siding with United Nations' decrees. The Patriot Act and TSA security procedures are, in my opinion, a training ground for U.S. citizens, designed to numb our sensitivities to government control. Once the rebels in America have been adequately neutered or spayed, the United Nations will simply demand compliance, with our own government's blessings. And the first item on their agenda will be the removal of firearms from your home.

Relocation of people into smart growth zones

The world's population is a critical area of concern for the United Nations' sustained development initiative, and while I recognize that many nations are not capable of supporting continued population growth, many of these limitations are the result of policy decisions and corruption, not the Earth's resources. But the United Nations tends to hold governments blameless in this area, and instead point the finger at families and lack of education as the culprit.

In yet another example of how governments, and the United Nations in particular, believe they know what is best for you, the United Nations has sponsored significant research in the area of population control. The goals of the United Nations' Population Fund "are an integral part of all efforts to achieve sustained and sustainable social and economic development that meets human needs, ensures well-being and protects the natural resources on which all life depends" (Population & Development Review, 1996). In other words, according to the United Nations, the best way to ensure sustainability of resources is to limit the world's population. The Population Fund goes on to list the means of achieving its population control goals, which primarily focus on family planning and birth control, and as recently as 2010 have enlisted the support of faith based organizations to spread their message of birth control (Karam, 2010).

In its seminal document on sustained development in America, the President's Council on Sustainable Development declares "the stabilization of the U.S. population" as one of its primary goals. This is interesting, given that the majority of population growth in this country is the result of immigration, both legal and illegal.

Beyond the drive to reduce the world's population, Agenda 21 takes a nastier turn in its effort to create "smart growth zones" in developed nations. In the United States, major metropolitan areas along the eastern and western seaboards will become stacked and packed mega-cities, allowing the removal of people from rural areas across the nation in a mass exodus that will make the Highland Clearances of the 18th and 19th centuries look like the eviction of a bachelor from his one room apartment.

Ironically, the movement of the nation's population into stacked and packed mega-cities will not be a significant shift in our population. According to the World Resource Institute, 75 percent of Americans live in urban areas, with over half of the population clustered around 39 cities of 1 million plus people. The Agenda 21 plan, which you may remember was being discussed by the Clinton Administration, is to simply move access to education, jobs, and healthcare to these urban areas, effectively forcing the majority of rural residents to "voluntarily" move. An additional technique to encourage urbanization will be the use of government incentives in the form of grants, tax credits, and government housing benefits. As they move, private property will be scooped up by the state in property condemnations and eminent domain seizures. For the stubborn rebels, the lack of access to essential services like police and fire protection will make it easy for marauders to prey on the holdouts, which will have the desired effect of either killing the resistant squatters, or burning them out.

If you don't think the mass relocation of rural Americans is possible, think of how the methods listed above worked to clear the hills during the Tennessee Valley Authority construction. But the most powerful eviction tool used by the government is the right of eminent domain. In a report titled "Public Power, Private Gain," the Institute for Justice has documented over 10,000 cases of eminent domain abuse, where property owners have faced forced removal from their land and home sites. The intent of eminent domain is to claim private property for public use, such as the construction of a freeway by-pass, or the expansion of a sewage treatment plant. However, as the cases documented by the Institute for Justice suggest, the government is now routinely working with developers and environmentalists to seize private property without justification.

Overseas this forced movement of people is also evident in the Yangtze River basin in China. Construction of the largest dam in the world has led to the destruction of entire cities, and the displacement of millions of people, most of whom moved from their rural farms to mega-cities like Shanghai. Sure, you can point to the advantages of the Yangtze Dam, but my point is, the government can contrive any justification necessary to remove you from your land or home. In the end, the stated objective of Agenda 21 is to see 50 percent of the landmass of the United States vacated and left to nature.

If the proponents of Agenda 21 achieve their goals, much of the land that currently comprises the bread basket of the world will be off limits to human habitation and activity. Furthermore, the rich farmlands of the San Joaquin and Imperial Valleys will become fallow as irrigation and water rights are restricted. Exactly what are we supposed to eat when we are holed up in tiny apartments in massive government housing units? Is the slow starvation of the masses their ultimate goal? Once the urbanization process has been completed, the final solution to the world's population problem will be within the reach of a simple command to "flip the switch."

"The good Lord set definite limits on man's wisdom, but set no limits on his stupidity - and that's just not fair."

Konrad Adenauer

Call to Action

While the bulk of this expose has focused on the actions of elected officials, the elephant in the corner of the room is actually a growing trend towards governing by rule of regulation. America is a nation of laws, and the elected officials in our state and federal legislative bodies have been given the authority to create those laws. Unfortunately, what is happening is that appointed officials from agencies across the nation are enacting rules and regulations that effectively circumvent the legislative process.

For example, Agenda 21 is not a law or a treaty enacted by Congress, and the President's Council on Sustainable Development is not an agency created by Congress. Yet, they have both resulted in significant regulations as well as imposition of controls on individual property rights. Presumably, if the United Nations, and the host of non-government organizations that champion its causes, succeeds in fully implementing Agenda 21, you will not recognize America.

In another example of ruling through regulation, the Endangered Species Act uses habitat protection as a means to set aside land currently accessible for recreational purposes, such as National Parks, deserts, and our forests into conservation districts, where any human activity is forbidden. In the Selway-Bitterroot wilderness areas strict laws governing the grazing of animals makes it illegal for a horse or pack animal to take a bite of grass within the wilderness area, which effectively makes thousands of square miles of beautiful land inaccessible to most people. And in the Mojave Desert strict rules regarding staying on trails makes it illegal for hikers and campers to experience the wide open expanses of the desert. Eventually, according to contributors to the Agenda 21 accord, up to 50 percent of all land in the United States will be off limits to human activity—and your representative in Congress will never cast a single vote for or against this action.

In a world where City Park Rangers tote assault rifles, private security firms are granted arrest powers, mobile naked body scanners cruise up and down streets prying into people's homes and vehicles, and emails and text messages are scanned by barricaded government eavesdroppers, there is no limit to the reach of the government. Government apologists routinely cite "the ends justify the means" as the justification for invasive police tactics and the usurpation of constitutional law by the very people sworn to defend the Constitution. But lest we forget, Adolf Hitler himself used the expression "the ends justify the means" dozens of times in his book, "Mein Kampf," and we all know where that got us.

Under no circumstances should a justification for an "ends" warrant blanket approval of any "means" possible. Rather, every action taken by a government must be tested against the natural laws of man. And in the case of the greatest nation every devised by man, the means must also meet the strict limits of constitutional law. Agenda 21 proponents will offer compelling arguments in favor of global sustained development, and on the surface they will sound reasonable. Consider these examples from my own personal experience…

As a child growing up near a cement plant, I remember how the air for miles around lay entrapped in a perpetual fog bank. Only this was not fog. It was a cloud of dust, heavy with poisons that killed every tree in the area and blocked the view of the sky and surrounding mountains. In the early 1970s air pollution filters were put into place. The air cleared, trees returned to life, and the plant continued to operate and make money for its stakeholders and employees.

Living in the Persian Gulf area in the 1990s I observed garbage trucks routinely dumping industrial waste in the waters. The beaches were a wreck and the surrounding waters too unpleasant to swim. The pearl industry suffered, fishing ground to a standstill, and tourism was non-existent. Over the past twenty plus years the local governments have realized the Gulf waters are a precious treasure, worth saving, and have made progress in reversing the tradition of using the ocean as a landfill.

Other environmental tragedies like the Exxon Valdez and BP oil spills suggest we have a ways to go yet, and learning how to prevent incidences of this nature are worthy causes. But at what cost? I part ways with the environmentalists when their zeal for reform begins to resemble eco-terrorism, and where the rights and needs of humanity must take a backseat to nature.

We face a host of pollution and sustained development challenges, but in my opinion many of these issues can be met with free market solutions. We do not need the bloated bureaucracy of the United Nations dictating policy at the national and local levels. Let them focus on hosting summit meetings that promote world peace, and leave the rest of us alone. Agenda 21 is a carefully disguised attempt to hijack the worthy cause of environmentalism in the pursuit of political objectives. As one signatory to the United Nations' General Assembly among at least 193 others, the initiatives being put into place in the name of sustained development represent a threat to our national sovereignty. If the citizenry of the various nations that prize freedom and self-governance do not resolve to stop the United Nations in its tracks, we will all be answering to the same handful of elites whose selfish pursuit of utopia will relegate the vast majority of the world's population to a life of servitude and limited opportunity.

It's time to relegate Agenda 21 to the dustbin of history, where it belongs.

"Freedom and democracy will leave Marxism and Leninism on the ash heap of history."

President Ronald Reagan

Author's Note

It should be noted that my criticism of Agenda 21 and its apparent goals are not directed towards individuals within the United Nations or the U.S. Government, and while the ballot box does not appear to be a viable way to derail this movement, please do not interpret my call to action as a call to arms. We must work together to find a peaceful and lawful way to resolve this apparent threat to our way of life.

Sharing information relevant to Agenda 21 is a step in that direction. The following text is based on my opinion, shaped by a careful reading of various United Nations and U.S. Government documents relevant to sustained development and their apparent goal of one world government rule.

"What use of thee can any creature make? For any good? What profit dost thou bring?"

Humphrey Mill "Of Darknesse" 1639

Notes

Municipal Environmental Policy in Norway: from 'mainstream' policy to 'real' Agenda 21? By: Aall, Carlo. Local Environment, Nov2000, Vol. 5 Issue 4, p451-465, 15p

Involving citizens in sustainable development: evidence of new forms of participation in the Danish Agenda 21 schemes. By: Agger, Annika. Local Environment, Jul2010, Vol. 15 Issue 6, p541-552, 12p

Karl Marx and the Tradition of Western Political Thought. By: Arendt, Hannah. Social Research, Summer2002, Vol. 69 Issue 2, p273-319, 47p

On Marx: An Introduction to the Revolutionary Intellect of Karl Marx. By: AU, WAYNE. Science & Society, Jan2010, Vol. 74 Issue 1, p133-135, 3p

The Right War. By: Ban Ki-moon. Time, 4/28/2008, Vol. 171 Issue 17, p58-58, 1p

Local Agenda 21 in Japan: transforming local environmental governance. By: Barrett, Brendan; Usui, Mikoto. Local Environment, Feb2002, Vol. 7 Issue 1, p49-67, 19p

CFACT. Committee For A Constructive Tomorrow. http://www.cfact.tv/2010/12/08/un-climate-kooks-want-to-cripple-us-economy-and-ban-h2o. Downloaded 10 December 2010.

Putting Young Old Ideas into Action: the relevance of Growing Up in Cities to Local Agenda 21. By: Chawla, Louise. Local Environment, Feb2001, Vol. 6 Issue 1, p13-25, 13p

Leave Politics Out of Climate Change. By: Chen Ying. Beijing Review, 5/24/2007, Vol. 50 Issue 21, p17-17, 1p

Assessing sustainability: An assessment framework to evaluate Agenda 21 actions at the local level. By: Corbière-Nicollier, Tourane; Ferrari, Yves; Jemelin, Christophe; Jolliet, Olivier. International Journal of Sustainable Development & World Ecology, Sep2003, Vol. 10 Issue 3, p225-237, 13p

Marx and the Mixed Economy: Money, Accumulation, and the Role of the State. By: DAVIS, ANN E. Science & Society, Jul2010, Vol. 74 Issue 3, p409-428, 20p

Global Health Priority Agenda for the 21st Century. By: Debas, Haile T. UN Chronicle, 2010, Vol. 47 Issue 2, p8-10, 3p

Does the IMF Help or Hurt? The Effect of IMF Programs on the Likelihood and Outcome of Currency Crises. By:

Dreher, Axel; Walter, Stefanie. World Development, Jan2010, Vol. 38 Issue 1, p1-18, 18p

The ISC framework: modelling drivers for the degree of Local Agenda 21 implantation in Western Europe. By: Echebarria, Carmen; Barrutialf, Jose M.; Aguado, Itziar. Environment & Planning A, Apr2009, Vol. 41 Issue 4, p980-995, 16p

Imagined citizens and participation: Local Agenda 21 in two communities in Sweden and Austria. By: Feichtinger, Judith; Pregernig, Michael. Local Environment, Jun2005, Vol. 10 Issue 3, p229-242, 14p

Surrender or resistance to the implementation of Local Agenda 21 in Portugal: the challenges of local governance for sustainable development. By: Fidélis, Teresa; Pires, Sara Moreno. Journal of Environmental Planning & Management, Jun2009, Vol. 52 Issue 4, p497-518, 22p

UN Oil for Food 'Scandal'. By: Gordon, Joy. Nation, 12/6/2004, Vol. 279 Issue 19, p27-28, 2p

All in the Family? U.N. Practices Under Scrutiny. By: Hosenball, Mark. Newsweek, 6/27/2005, Vol. 145 Issue 26, p9-10, 2p

Democratic and Environmental Effects of Local Agenda 21: a comparative analysis over time. By: Joas, Marko. Local Environment, May2001, Vol. 6 Issue 2, p213-221, 9p

Presidential Policy Directive on Global Development. **https://www.fas.org/irp/offdocs/ppd/global-dev.pdf**. Downloaded 18 December 2013.

Leonard, A., The Story of Cap and Trade. http://storyofstuff.com/capandtrade. Downloaded 17 December 2010

Local Agenda 21 and Barriers to Sustainability at the Local Government Level in Victoria, Australia. By: Mercer, David; Jotkowitz, Benjamin. Australian Geographer, Jul2000, Vol. 31 Issue 2, p163-181, 19p

The United Nations Population Fund's (UNFPA's) Legacy of Engaging Faith-Based Organizations as Cultural Agents of Change. By: Karam, Azza. Cross Currents, Sep2010, Vol. 60 Issue 3, p432-450, 19p

The Plan To Have the U.N. Rule. By: McManus, John F.. Vital Speeches of the Day, 2/15/2002, Vol. 68 Issue 9, p264, 6p

Sustainable Forestry in Thailand: The Effect of Agenda 21 on Forest-Related Non-Governmental Organizations. By: Mohlenkamp, Matthew J.. Pacific Affairs, Fall2003, Vol. 76 Issue 3, p427-442, 16p

Glorification, Disillusionment or the Way into the Future? The significance of Local Agenda 21 processes for the needs of local sustainability. By: Moser, Peter. Local Environment, Nov2001, Vol. 6 Issue 4, p453-467, 15p

Trust, cooperation, and implementation of sustainability programs: The case of Local Agenda 21. By: Owen, Ann L.; Videras, Julio. Ecological Economics, Dec2008, Vol. 68 Issue 1/2, p259-272, 14p

Meeting the challenges of Agenda 21: Priorities for the science and technology community. By: Pillay, Dorsamy; Rosswall, Thomas; Glaser, Gisbert. South African Journal of Science, Jul/Aug2002, Vol. 98 Issue 7/8, p331-333, 3p

Population Goals of the United Nations. Population & Development Review, Sep96, Vol. 22 Issue 3, p594-600, 7p

The IMF on the Global Crisis and Its Resolution. By: Rakshit, Mihir. Development & Change, Nov2009, Vol. 40 Issue 6, p1293-1307, 15p

Participating or Just Talking? Sustainable Development Councils and the Implementation of Agenda 21. By: Rosenberg, Jonathan; Thomas, Linus Spencer. Global Environmental Politics, May2005, Vol. 5 Issue 2, p61-87, 27p

Local agenda 21 in Italy: an effective governance tool for facilitating local communities' participation and promoting capacity building for sustainability. By: Sancassiani, Walter. Local Environment, Apr2005, Vol. 10 Issue 2, p189-200, 12p

Schlafly, P. The U.S. Should Halt All Funding For U.N.'s 'Global Warming' Scam. http://www.investors.com/NewsAndAnalysis/Article.aspx?id=556625&p=2. Downloaded 14 December 2010.

Public Participation and Policy: unpacking connections in one UK Local Agenda 21. By: Sharp, Liz. Local Environment, Feb2002, Vol. 7 Issue 1, p7-22, 16p

Towards indicators for institutional sustainability: lessons from an analysis of Agenda 21. By: Spangenberg, Joachim H.; Pfahl, Stefanie; Deller, Kerstin. Ecological Indicators, Nov2002, Vol. 2 Issue 1/2, p61, 17p

Local agenda 21, capacity building and the cities of Peru. By: Steinberg, Florian; Miranda, Liliana. Habitat International, Mar2005, Vol. 29 Issue 1, p163-182, 20p

Sustainable Development in Thailand: Lessons From Implementing Local Agenda 21 in Three Cities. By: Tonami, Aki; Mori, Akihisa. Journal of Environment & Development, Sep2007, Vol. 16 Issue 3, p269-289, 21p

The UN 'Scandal' Report. By: Williams, Ian. Nation, 2/28/2005, Vol. 280 Issue 8, p6-21, 2p

Earth Summits approves Agenda 21, Rio Declaration record number of world leaders attend. United Nations Chronicle, Sep92, Vol. 29 Issue 3, p59, 7p

Skycap scam discovered at Miami International Airport. By Jade Walker. Yahoo News. http://news.yahoo.com/s/yblog_spoint/20101118/ts_yblog _spoint/skycap-scam-discovered-at-miami-international-airport. Downloaded 18 Nov 2010.

Role of the IMF in the Global Financial Crisis. By: Xafa, Miranda. CATO Journal, Fall2010, Vol. 30 Issue 3, p475-489, 15p

A Scandal Heats Up. By: Zagorin, Adam. Time, 5/16/2005, Vol. 165 Issue 20, p17-17, 1/2p

Appendix: The 2030 Agenda

Who among us does not want to end poverty and improve the health and safety of all humans?

The creators of the United Nations' 2030 Agenda understand this, and propose and implement their globalization and one world government plans in the language of idealistic reformers—that is, in the language of health, safety, and justice for all, devoid of consequences or ramifications.

And in the tradition of generations of reformers and idealistic dreamers, they forget that while we all share the same planet, we are individuals. We value privacy, personal freedoms, traditions, and yes, our national identities.

Simply put, humans cannot be collected, boxed, and controlled like a colony of bees. Nor can we be transplanted and husbanded like ants in a child's terrarium.

During the summer months of 2015, leading up to the September 2015 United Nations General Assembly, members of the United Nations met in Addis Ababa to draft a resolution of sweeping and all-inclusive goals for the world they formally called *Transforming Our World: The 2030 Agenda for Sustainable Development*.

The 2030 Agenda represents an extension of the Agenda 21's focus on the environment into the social, economic, and political realms of nations. Essentially, the 2030 Agenda is the embodiment of four foundational United Nations documents:

- The Universal Declaration of Human Rights

- The Millennium Declaration

- The 2005 World Summit Outcome

- The Declaration on the Right to Development

Using these foundational documents as guide stones, the drafters of the 2030 Agenda resolution created 17 specific goals, ranging from the eradication of poverty and hunger, to the realization of gender equality and global unification. Here are the goals…

Goal 1: End global poverty.

Goal 2: Fight global hunger.

Goal 3: Deliver universal health care

Goal 4: Ensure global educational equality.

Goal 5: Achieve gender equality.

Goal 6: Provide sustainable water and sanitation to all.

Goal 7: Ensure global access to sustainable energy resources.

Goal 8: Promote economic growth and full employment.

Goal 9: Improve infrastructures and sustainable industrialization worldwide.

Goal 10: Reduce inequality within and among countries.

Goal 11: Make cities safe.

Goal 12: Manage consumption and production patterns.

Goal 13: Reduce the impact of climate change.

Goal 14: Conserve marine resources for sustainable development.

Goal 15: Protect, restore and promote sustainable use of ecosystems.

Goal 16: Promote peaceful societies and ensure global access to justice.

Goal 17: Revitalize the global partnership for sustainable development.

As you can see, the 17 stated goals of the 2030 Agenda appears benign; however, as Adolf Hitler preached in his *Mein Kampf*, the ends justify the means. In this case, the United Nations has proposed 169 sub-goals in the 2030 Agenda, which in my opinion pose a clear and present danger to American sovereignty and your natural rights, beginning with its collectivist values.

Collectivism and the United Nations

The United Nations is a collective of leaders and diplomats from around the world, and by definition, any initiative conceived and delivered by the United Nations is steeped in its collectivist values.

Collectivism puts society and government above the individual, and has no qualms with sacrificing individual freedoms for the common good. Ironically, the most effective way to instill collectivist values is to create or capitalize on tragedy…as this proves the need for increased government intervention, in the name of security for all.

We've seen this in America, where post 9/11 security measures have seen the rise of the TSA, the Patriot Act, and the annihilation of privacy rights. Proponents of these security measures claim government intrusion into our lives saves lives, and refuting the validity of their security measures places opponents of intrusive government snooping and blatant disregard for individual rights in the position of proving a negative.

That is, the federal government can point to weapons like toenail clippers and water bottles confiscated by airline security personnel as proof their efforts are saving lives since tragedies comparable to those of 9/11 have been averted. In order to challenge the validity of these security measures, you would have to prove the TSA does little, if anything, to prevent terrorism in the skies.

Proving a negative reminds me of the story of a man who spent the better part of his life beating a drum and chanting nonsense in Times Square.

"What are you doing?" a tourist once asked the deranged man.

"Keeping giraffes from attacking the streets of New York City," the man answered as he danced and chanted.

"Dancing and chanting won't keep giraffes off the streets," the tourist replied.

"Oh yeah?" the giraffe hater said. "Have you seen any giraffes on the streets of New York?"

Foiled by logic and the futility of trying to prove a negative, the tourist shook his head and went on his way, confident the city was safe from giraffe attack.

The 2030 Agenda is comparable to chasing imaginary giraffes, and epitomizes the collective movement as it calls upon individuals to set aside their ambitions, to forfeit their natural rights, and to subjugate themselves to the state—presumably in the interest of 17 lofty goals, that incidentally position the goal creators to anoint themselves as your caretaker and keeper. And like the giraffe hating chanter, it's all good...after all, according to the collectivists, the state knows what is good for you, and is the best guardian of your future.

The 2030 Agenda poses a real threat to life as you know it, as the United Nations' purported attempts to secure the peace and provide for domestic tranquility and equality for all is intoxicating because it plays on Maslow's instinctive human need for security above all other desires.

During a Bilderberger conference in 1991, Henry Kissinger alluded to the cry for national security as the gateway to globalization. That is, when faced with threats such as famine, plague, and terrorism, free people will willingly cast off their freedoms and embrace tyranny, if only their new keepers can assure them safety.

That is what the United Nations, in my opinion, is attempting to accomplish in its 2030 Agenda. In a world balanced on the precipice of dramatic and uncertain change, the 17 goals discussed in this text are like Reagan's shining city on the hill. To the ill-informed and the disenfranchised, the goals are a beacon of hope. But to the critical thinkers and freedom lovers amongst us, they are the all-embracing and tyrannical arms of the nanny state—guided by a coven of elites who will never live by the restricted standards and forfeited rights they impose on its willing subjects.

Again, who among us does not want to end poverty and improve the health and safety of all humans?

In my opinion, both the stated and unstated goals of the United Nations represent a "bridge too far." The 17 goals of the 2030 Agenda epitomizes hubris and government overreach. And education, critical thinking, and the election of leaders committed to upholding their sworn duty to our constitution is the only way to slow or stop its implementation and the eventual forfeiture of our sovereign rights.

And make no mistake…America is the crown jewel in the globalists' eyes. They covet our wealth and despise our freedoms, and where they fail to lift third world countries out of abject poverty and unchecked violence, they will attempt to achieve global equality and level the playing field by taking us down.

In the United Nations' own words, "Never before have world leaders pledged common action and endeavor across such a broad and universal policy agenda" (United Nations, 2015). Leading the way in this "common action" is the United Nations' war on poverty.

The War on Poverty

In a speech before the United Nations General Assembly on 1 October, 2015, Israeli Prime Minister Benjamin Netanyahu stated, "The best intentions do not prevent the worst outcomes." Netanyahu was referring to the Iran nuclear deal in his statement, but in a broader sense, he was referring to a tradition within the United Nations of rewarding bad behavior, and specifically referenced a history of the United Nations condemning Israel while ignoring the atrocities in neighboring Syria.

Netanyahu's speech illustrates exactly how the feckless policy makers within the United Nations can take the best plans and best intentions, and turn them into a disaster. Sadly, embedded within the 2030 Agenda are countless opportunities for this ineffectual international organization to inflict body blows to American sovereignty and your rights as it strives to solidify its position in global politics.

Its quest for global governance begins with its "War on Poverty."

According to the 2030 Agenda, the United Nations defines poverty as people living on less than $1.25 per day. It is unclear from their definition if this means "per person" or "per household." Either way, the stated goal to end global poverty aims to cut the poverty rate in half by 2030, which stands at an estimated 1.4 billion as of 2015.

To achieve this goal, the United Nations has identified six specific steps it will take (United Nations, 2015):

1. Implement social protection systems to apparently offer physical security as well as possibly welfare type safety nets.

2. Ensure vulnerable populations are given equal access to economic resources.

3. Reduce the impact of climate related disasters on vulnerable populations.

4. Mobilize a significant increase in resource allocation to poverty stricken areas.

5. Accelerate investments in various poverty eradication actions.

6. And finally, develop policy frameworks at the national, regional and international levels aimed at eliminating poverty.

Prior to 2015 the United Nations set 2015 as a deadline to reduce global poverty by half. During its 2015 review of progress in this area, the United Nations proclaimed victory on the "War on Poverty" front, and admitted much of the progress was attributable to "an unprecedented ramp-up in aid from rich countries to poor ones" (Nurith, 2015).

Currently, the United Nations expects developed nations to dedicate over .7 percent (seven tenths of a percent) of their respective gross national incomes to foreign aid. It doesn't sound like much, but in America alone, this amounts to over $124 billion per year, or $375 per person.

Given the lofty goals of the 2030 Agenda, this number will see a substantial increase over the next decade. However, the United Nations sees its 2030 Agenda goals challenged by the lack of political will to "step up" to the necessary funding of poverty and hunger relief funding requirements over the next 15 years.

In fact, during an *All Things Considered* interview on NPR, a top United Nations official, Amina Mohammed, claimed the billions of dollars spent thus far on eradicating poverty was insufficient, and further stated, "What this **agenda** needs to do is to move from billions to trillions" (Nurith, 2015).

In other words, we need to expand the redistribution of wealth from the developed nations to third world nations by at least 100 times.

These challenges exemplify my point that you cannot "buy" your way out of poverty. In a way, simply throwing money into a third world economy and falsely inflating local economies and daily pay rates is tantamount to feeding a man a fish, as opposed to teaching him to fish for himself.

Many Americans see the funding of poverty eradication programs overseas as a worthwhile cause, but what about its impact on our local economies and our way of life? What would an additional $124 billion per year spent on social programs, housing, research and development, and infrastructure do for America? Or, in the spirit of Amina Mohammed's ambitious request, $1 trillion?

To put this in perspective, consider how much is currently being spent on domestic programs in the United States...

- NASA receives approximately $18 billion per year in funding. (Hartman, 2010)

- The Supplemental Nutrition Assistance Program, also known as Food Stamps, spends approximately $74 billion per year. (House Food Stamp Bill Summary and Cost Estimates, 2013)

- The Congressional Budget Office (CBO) estimates that Medicare spending for prescription drugs under Part D will cost taxpayers $76 billion in 2015.

Medicare accounts for 22% of all spending on health care services in America and represents a huge chunk of our federal budget, with annual costs approaching $600 billion. (Johnson, et al, 2013)

- Within the discretionary spending portion of the federal budget, we spend $70 billion on education, $26 billion on transportation, and $39 billion on a combined category of energy and the environment.

Given the above numbers, it is clear the American taxpayers are more than generous with their current contributions to various United Nations' programs. However, as Amina Mohammed suggests above, enough is never enough, and what we do give, disappears like a cup of water poured onto a sand dune.

As previous failures in poverty eradication, such as Make Poverty History and countless United Nations' initiatives suggest, platitudes and resolutions will get you nowhere. But the last thing any parent wants to see is a starving child, and many Americans see world hunger as a true tragedy…as evidenced by our generous donations of food and money to developing nations.

But the apparent corruption and hypocrisy rife within the United Nations' efforts to end hunger never ceases to amaze me.

Have you ever seen the anti-American sentiment among workers unloading trucks laden with bags of rice or wheat with "Gift from the American People" stenciled on each bag? Or watched as millions of dollars in donated food and money disappears into black holes around the globe?

In my opinion, the distribution of food and money to developing nations should be handled by charitable organizations, with their representatives on the ground, ensuring that every grain of wheat or rice given by American citizens finds its way into a starving child's mouth, and not the black market.

Yet, the United Nations knows what is best…including how to evoke gender equality, even as half their members practice blatant discrimination against women.

Creating Gender Equality

There was a time, not too long ago, when women's rights advocates fought for equality by demanding the right to vote, the right to work and equal pay, and freedom from discrimination.

Now, the fight for rights has shifted to a fight to punish and take away rights from men.

This effort is in keeping with the tenets of the 2030 Agenda, which apparently aims to achieve equality, not by lifting the downtrodden up, but by bringing those with presumed privilege down.

For example, in the world of federal contracting there are two essential elements that any viable contract offer must meet: responsiveness and responsibility.

A responsive contract offer simply means the bid or offer was submitted on time, and in the proper format. Whereas, a responsible offer is one the contracting officers believe the contractor is capable of delivering. That is, capable of honoring or completing in accordance with the terms of the contract.

The equal rights movement in federal contracting has never suggested (to my knowledge) that unresponsive bids should be accepted; however, in the subjective world of responsibility, contracting officials are given considerable leeway to assess the ability of various contractors…which gives them the authority to accept bids, regardless of price, from so-called "protected" interests like minorities and women.

Another tool at the contracting officer's disposal is a point system that awards contracts based on points awarded to contractors in the bidding process. It's like a fantasy football system, where a contractor wins points by being responsive, offering a fair price, guaranteeing the contracted work will be performed by a diverse team of employees, and whether or not the contracting firm is owned by a minority, a female, or in some cases, a veteran.

Again, like in fantasy football, the highest points are accrued by "stacking." In the case of winning a federal contract, a company owned by a black female veteran will beat a comparable bid by a company owned by a white male.

This drive to win equality by punishing men is dangerous because it introduces social engineering and outcome based assessment rules into the free market—potentially harming innovation as well as the strength of our small business community. It's essentially management by objectives, where the objective is a predetermined decision to control the contract selection process outside the scope of meritocracy.

Small business is the backbone of the American economy, and any regulatory action that impacts the small business owner, impacts main street America. According to the 2014 U.S. Industry & Market Outlook report, of the 28,000 firms and establishments surveyed, 23,000 have less than 4 employees (Barnes Report, 2014); clearly indicating the vital role small business plays in the American economy.

Yet, with initiatives and goals espoused by the 2030 Agenda, our intrepid leaders want to decimate entrepreneurship.

While most businesses in America employ fewer than 4 people, contracting law and gender equality movements comparable to the 2030 Agenda, insist employers maintain a diverse workforce. In the case of a local electrical company competing for a contact to repair the wiring in an Air Force hangar for example, the small firm may be required to hire a minority and/or a female before winning the contract.

Now, there is absolutely nothing wrong with hiring a minority or a female. If you need a new employee, and a qualified applicant comes along who happens to be black, or female, so what? Hire the person.

But, these affirmative action initiatives are harmful when they manipulate statistics to satisfy means testing in the interest of fairness. Hiring a female just to check a box does nothing to promote or realize gender equality, and in fact may set the movement back by inciting hatred for equal rights programs, and in the case of a small business, winning a government contract may mean firing a qualified employee to make room for the affirmative action hire—which ironically, undermines the United Nations' goals to stimulate economic growth.

Stimulate Economic Growth

One of the biggest hypocrisies in the United Nations' 2030 Agenda is its quest for economic growth.

But in my opinion, long before the United Nations can tell us and the global community at large how to develop and sustain its economies, it must first learn how to "practice what is preaches" by improving its transparency and eliminating graft and corruption within its own ranks.

Is corruption the "order of the day" at the United Nations? Apparently, while this monolithic global legislative body claims to know what is best for us, and touts an endless stream of cooperative agreements and feel-good projects, it is not above simple human greed.

Despite United Nations General Assembly President Mogens Lykketoft's assertion that "there is no place" for corruption within the United Nations, evidence suggests scandal after scandal, such as the Iraqi oil for food program, and more recently allegations of bribery for favoritism and access to top United Nations' officials, is an ongoing "business as usual" affair (FoxNews, 2015).

The preponderance of the evidence against the United Nations is daunting and suggests an order of the day that makes Chicago style politics look like grade school playground antics.

How can an organization noted for scandal and repeated failures aspire to represent the high moral ground on issues like poverty, hunger, and equality? In my opinion, it doesn't care. Its prime directive is not driven by altruistic humanitarianism…but rather, the overt control of a one world government. And since the United States represents the chokepoint in its global ambitions, the annihilation of our social, economic, and political systems is a prerequisite to the United Nations' rise to global domination.

Again, are these the guys you want running the world? And what are the chances they can really bring equality and economic growth to the entire world? These thugs are convinced they have some kind of mandate from God, but in reality, they're just a modern day version of the Gang That Couldn't Shoot Straight.

Beyond the confines of the top brass in the General Assembly, try to imagine how a single tax dollar will be used to level the economic playing field around the world. The first thing you should consider is the number of offices and management levels your dollar will have to navigate before finding its way out of the United Nations and into the hands of local government officials. From there it would have to traverse a labyrinth of bureaucracies and their attendant bureaucrats before finding its way to shovel ready projects.

At this point you may be thinking of the 2008 financial crisis and how billions of dollars were going to be spent to fund shovel ready projects. The logic was simple, if you pour cash into construction projects, contractors will hire people, and employed people will spend money shopping.

But there is nothing logical or predictable about local government authorities. It did not work in America, and it will not work in developing nations. The recipients of any economic stimulant packages will have their own pet projects to promote, brothers-in-laws to appease, and village elders to bribe.

In the end, if a single penny of your tax dollar finds its way out of the United Nations and into the hands of a peasant in some remote village south of the dark side of the moon, it will be a miracle.

Ultimately, the only predictable result of any United Nations' attempt to spur economic growth will be a land rush for Florida condominiums and Italian built sports cars from a very select crowd of nouveau rich...leaving the carpet bombing of remote villages with dollar bills a less expensive and more effective strategy.

Either way, the United Nations would succeed by simply redistributing the wealth of the developed nations to the more deserving warlords of the developing nations.

You lose...they win. Worst of all, this will all be accomplished with the aid and blessings of our elected representatives...the same ones who manage our states and cities.

Invoking Peaceful Coexistence

While visiting the City of Brotherly Love (Philadelphia) in September 2015, Pope Francis declared, "God is living in our cities." I guess he never visited Germantown or Strawberry Mansion after sunset, or reflected on his own experiences in the slum cities of Argentina where he grew up. Then again, Pope Francis is not stupid or naïve. In my opinion, he knows exactly what is going on in cities around the world, and is bartering with the only currency he possesses…hope and faith.

I suppose hope and faith will come in handy the next time a flash mob throws bricks through my windshield in West Philadelphia. And I suppose because the United Nations wrote some pretty words about making cities safe by 2030, the drug lords, gangs, and incompetent government officials controlling our cities will come to Jesus and change their evil ways.

Sadly, the predominant perpetrators of violence in our cities will never hear of the 2030 Agenda, and may not even be cognizant of the United Nations' role in shaping international policy. All they will see is an increased police presence on their streets, and the continuance of modern day equivalents (free phones, food stamps, housing, etc.) of the failed Roman strategy to offer free bread to placate the masses and discourage social unrest.

Short of government subsidized and sponsored economic opportunity programs, entrepreneurs will continue to avoid the inner cities like the plague; and capitalism, the bane of both the United Nations and the Vatican, will take its curative dollars elsewhere, leaving community organizers to cry "injustice" as the voters they covet stumble from one failed social engineering project to another.

John Locke once stated, "The people cannot delegate to government the power to do anything which would be unlawful for them to do themselves." Yet every time we expose ourselves to stop and frisk activities on our streets or in our airports, or permit government agencies to enact and enforce regulations that supersede laws enacted by our elected representatives, we are subjected to government activities that you and I as individuals cannot do…including writing secretive trade pacts and shipping American jobs overseas.

The Hypocrisy of Free Trade

One of the more obvious anomalies in the world of economic equality is free trade. Long before NAFTA and the Trans Pacific Partnership became household names for pillaging the manufacturing sector of the U.S. economy, I wrote to my congressman and asked a simple question: How does a man in a developing nation offer economic opportunity for American manufacturers when he earns less than $1.25 per day?

My congressman's terse reply read like an executive summary of the United Nations' position on free trade. He was in their bag, and tried to sell me a bill of goods on how American companies and their respective employees would benefit from tariff free access to American products.

Right. After feeding and housing his family, a laborer earning around $30 per month was going to purchase an automobile made in Detroit, or perhaps log onto Amazon to purchase the latest New York bestseller.

It never happened…and it never will happen.

The harsh reality of free trade, as I see it, is the exportation of manufacturing jobs in America to sweat shops across Asia and Latin America, leaving the only viable outcome of any United Nations' driven initiative in this area to the suppression of opportunity and income in America to achieve contrived economic equality.

Sure, the American consumer enjoys comparatively inexpensive toys like cell phones, laptops, and televisions made in China, and clothing from Sri Lanka and Bangladesh. But what is the true price of these goods?

During the past 15 years, the median income in America has dropped by 20% in some Midwestern states, with average declines of 10-15% in 35 other states (Prall, 2013). Real employment levels in America have also taken a hit during this same time period. According to the Bureau of Labor Statistics, reported unemployment levels hover around 5% as of August 2015. However, the real unemployment rate, which accounts for those unemployed and those who have quit looking for work, is 12.6%.

In real numbers, 94 million Americans over the age of 16 are neither employed nor listed as unemployed (DeSilver, 2014), and according to the Bureau of Labor Statistics, the current participation rate in working Americans is the lowest it has been since 1977. Additionally, the number of Americans who rely on food stamp assistance continues to grow at record levels, with over 46 million Americans receiving assistance (Berry, 2015).

Another by-product of free trade, in my opinion, is the transition of minimum wage jobs from part time and entry level work, to full time career jobs. As a result, we have essentially become a nation of shopkeepers, flipping each other's burgers and washing each other's laundry...as well as a nation of protestors performing unskilled labor, while demanding pay rates comparable to the former union scale jobs many of us enjoyed in the previous century.

Third world diplomats and developed nation do-gooders in the barricaded offices of the United Nations must be wringing their hands in glee at the prospects of economic collapse in America. And rather than support or protect the economic crown jewel on this planet, they commit unsportsmanlike conduct by piling on with further restrictions to our growth... and now, even concocting plans for controlling consumption using Orwellian words like "sustainable" and "equal."

During a press conference on 2 October, 2015, President Obama stated, "Until we can get the warring parties on the ground to live together peacefully, no amount of military intervention will end conflict." Nor, I would add, will his efforts to organize the global community in the model of Chicago eliminate tribal and territorial violence.

Despite this simple truth about human nature, the United Nations wants us to believe that world peace can be assured by the presence of blue helmeted soldiers, food handouts, and manufactured economic opportunity. It won't work, and will only bleed more blood and treasure from America.

After 60 plus years of programs and billions of dollars in foreign aid, countless summit meetings and conferences, and decades of intervention, millions of refugees from places like Africa, the Middle East, and the Sub-Continent continue to risk their lives to cross oceans and evade political gangs to find a new life in Europe and America.

It's been said this is the greatest mass migration of people since World War II—and it is indicative of the United Nations' inability to prevent oppression, poverty, or hunger in the global community. The cultural, religious, and political rifts between warring tribes, sects, and nationalities in these regions are profound, and no amount of money or dialogue will ever change that.

Instead, the United Nations encourages sovereign nations to find homes for these refugees, with many of the loudest voices coming from representatives of nations with zero immigration policies (e.g. Saudi Arabia, Vatican City). In the fall of 2015, Germany agreed to accept 1 million refugees, and in America, the U.S. government spoke in terms of accepting 200,000 refugees (above and beyond its already generous immigration policy).

The current global immigration crisis is indicative of human nature, as people naturally flee violence and inequality, in search of opportunity and safety.

As a country boy growing up in the American Deep South, I used to think the best way to get rid of fire ants was to kick their raised mounds.

"All you're doing is scattering them," my dad would complain.

And he was right. Within days of "destroying" a fire ant mound, half a dozen new mounds would dot the area around the former ant hill.

To a certain degree, opening our borders to refugees is comparable to spreading the problem, rather than solving it. Of course, we can't eradicate the problem the way a farmer may choose to get rid of invasive ants, but we should understand that to follow the United Nations' plan of setting up refugee camps and welcoming millions of new people into our communities is tantamount to cultural and national suicide.

Yet, in my opinion, this is exactly what the power elite want to happen. From the early days of television sitcoms, to forced busing and the rise of political correctness, there has been a calculated campaign to destroy America from within by perverting and tweaking what is known as the "cultural literacy" of the nation. The current immigration and refugee crisis is just another chapter in a long book of how to destroy western civilization, and as this United Nations' 2030 Agenda goal clearly suggests, changing the demographics of a developed nation via mass migration is the quickest and easiest way to achieve a collectivist goal.

American Exceptionalism and the Road Ahead

Life is about choices. America is at a crossroads, where we can choose to follow the expedient and politically correct route of subservience to the United Nations and its collectivist values, or the isolationist's route steeped in our reverence for individualism and exceptionalism.

America is blessed with rich natural resources, but there is more to our success than mineral deposits and fertile farmland. The globalists don't get this…or if they do, they choose to ignore it. Instead, they choose to believe the wealth of this nation can lift the world's poor and hungry out of their collective misery.

It won't work. You can't buy yourself out of poverty without first instilling the values of innovation, private property, individual freedoms, hard work, capitalism, and democracy among the people.

Sadly, most of the world's poor are bereft of hope, and no amount of money or government intervention can cure disparity. I'm reminded of Winston Churchill's writings in the two volume unabridged version of *The River Wars*, where he refers to a "fearful fatalistic apathy" among the world's poor.

In Churchill's case, he blames the poverty of nations on religion (specifically Islam), but in fairness, there is plenty of poverty to go around…with or without Islam. But how does one explain generations of poverty stricken people stumbling over gold and diamonds? And how do you explain the lack of development in places rich in human potential and natural resources?

The United Nations explains third world poverty by pointing an accusatory finger at imperialism, slavery, and now, "white privilege."

Diplomats assigned to the United Nations building in New York City must stare in bewilderment and lust at the exceptionalism of America. And while they'll never understand it or duplicate it, they can occasionally "trip over nuts" as they organize summit meetings, write laws, and enact treaties.

That they can do. And that is the danger of the 2030 Agenda, as our misguided representatives will defy the will of the people and the Constitution they swore to protect and preserve to ratify it.

But take heart, the 2030 Agenda is doomed to fail.

I would never wish famine or genocide on any peoples, but I see hope in the gross incompetence of various United Nations agencies and programs. Notably, while assuming the mantle of global governance, the United Nations has failed to stem the growth of global terrorism or nuclear proliferation, and its record on humanitarian issues such as poverty, hunger, and genocide, severely curtails its moral authority.

These are just a handful of documented failures within the United Nations. And yet, they have set a deadline of 2030 for 17 specific goals...and the eventual assumption of rule under a one world government. You have to give them credit, they think big.

But honestly, short of America's complete capitulation to their goals, it will never happen.

That said, as I detailed in *Agenda 21*, many of the ineffectual programs and initiatives implemented by the United Nations trickle down and impact our lives at the local level, such as in carbon emissions and industrial growth restrictions that see valuable manufacturing jobs moved offshore…where ironically, government oversight and lack of regulatory control virtually guarantees even worse abuses to the environment.

It's up to us to stay the course, generously support humanitarian relief where we can, and continue to defend our sovereignty and individual rights…without the help of a one world government.

Here's the bottom line, in my opinion…

Lack of opportunity, equality, and the absence of peace in the world is not the fault of capitalism or American values. Instead, many of the world's problems stem from government corruption and a distinct lack of respect for human dignity. These are things you simply cannot legislate away. National pride, loyalty to your faith, and an instinctive drive to succeed runs deep among the majority of us. It is what defines us as individuals, and it is what binds communities and nations together.

That's how the real world works. And until we eliminate individuality, nationalism, and human motivation, the goals expressed in the 2030 Agenda will remain nothing but diplomatic pipe dreaming.

In my opinion, the United Nations knows this…which is why their success demands the eradication of both nation states and the human drive inherent in American Exceptionalism to rise above the masses.

Agenda 30 Resources

Barnes Reports: U.S. Offices of Real Estate Appraisers Industry. (2014). *United States Offices of Real Estate Appraisers Industry Report*, 1-232.

Berry, S. (2015). Gallup Ignores All-Time High Food Stamp Usage As Reason For 7-Year Low Percentage Americans Struggling To Afford Food. **http://www.breitbart.com/big-government/2015/06/07/gallup-ignores-all-time-high-food-stamp-usage-as-reason-for-7-year-low-percentage-americans-struggling-to-afford-food**. Accessed 10/02/2105.

Colglazier, W. (2015). Sustainable development agenda: 2030. *Science, 349*(6252), 1048-1050.

DeSilver, D. (2014). More and more Americans are outside the labor force entirely. Who are they? *Pew Research Center.* **http://www.pewresearch.org/fact-tank/2014/11/14/more-and-more-americans-are-outside-the-labor-force-entirely-who-are-they/** Accessed 9/26/2105.

FoxNews. (2015). 'No place at the United Nations': Ex-UN General Assembly leader accused of pocketing $500,000 in bribes. **http://www.foxnews.com/world/2015/10/06/us-investigating-alleged-united-nations-bribery-scheme/?intcmp=hplnws**. Accessed 10/06/2015.

Hartman, C. N. (2010). Projections for Future Funding of NASA And NASA Science Activities: Reassessing the Obama FY 2010 Budget Request. *AIP Conference Proceedings, 1208*(1), 454-463.

House Food Stamp Bill Summary and Cost Estimates. (2013). *Congressional Digest, 92*(9), 14-32.

Johnson, N. B., Losey, S., McElhatton, J., Medici, A., & Reily, S. (2013). The White House's 2014 budget request: agency by agency. *Federal Times, 49*(6), 10-12.

Nurith A. The World Could Wipe Out Extreme Poverty By 2030. There's Just One Catch. *All Things Considered (NPR)* [serial online]. July 13, 2015

Prall, D. (2013). Median household income holds steady. *American City & County Exclusive Insight*, 1.

United Nations. (2015). Transforming our world: the 2030 Agenda for Sustainable Development. **https://sustainabledevelopment.un.org/post2015/transfo rmingourworld**. Accessed 10/03/2015.

"We shall have World Government, whether or not we like it. The only question is whether World Government will be achieved by conquest or consent."

James Warburg

February 17th, 1950

Printed in Great Britain
by Amazon

26140423R00056